KT-457-662

Destination Detectives

France

North America

Europe

Asia

FRANCE

Africa

South America

Australasia

Paul Mason

Raintree

www.raintreepublishers.co.uk

Visit our website to find out more information about **Raintree** books.

To order:

☎ Phone 44 (0) 1865 888112

▤ Send a fax to 44 (0) 1865 314091

▤ Visit the Raintree Bookshop at **www.raintreepublishers.co.uk** to browse our catalogue and order online.

First published in Great Britain by
Raintree, Halley Court, Jordan Hill,
Oxford OX2 8EJ, part of Harcourt Education.
Raintree is a registered trademark of Harcourt
Education Ltd.

© Harcourt Education Ltd 2006
The moral right of the proprietor has been asserted.

All rights reserved. No part of this publication
may be reproduced, stored in a retrieval system,
or transmitted in any form or by any means,
electronic, mechanical, photocopying, recording,
or otherwise, without either the prior written
permission of the publishers or a licence permitting
restricted copying in the United Kingdom issued by
the Copyright Licensing Agency Ltd, 90 Tottenham
Court Road, London W1T 4LP (www.cla.co.uk).

Editorial: Melanie Copland and Lucy Beevor
Design: Victoria Bevan and Kamae Design
Picture Research: Hannah Taylor and Kay Altwegg
Production: Duncan Gilbert

Originated by Dot Gradations Ltd, UK
Printed and bound in China
by WKT Company Limited

ISBN 1 844 2140 79
10 09 08 07 06
10 9 8 7 6 5 4 3 2 1

British Library Cataloguing in Publication Data
Mason, Paul
France. – (Destination detectives)
944'.084
A full catalogue record for this book is available from
the British Library.

Acknowledgements

Alamy Images pp. 9 (Agence Images), 35 (Directphoto.org), 34r
(images-of-france), 6b (Jack Sullivan), 41 (Jon Arnold Images), 20
(Justin Kase), 13 (mediacolors), 32 (Nick Hanna), 10 (Travel Ink),
7 (Westend61); Anthony Blake Photo Library pp. 16–17 (Gerrit
Buntrock), 17 (Robert Golden); Corbis pp. 18–19 (Bryan F.
Peterson), pp. 24r, 26 (Chris Lisle), 33 (Dave G. Houser), 37
(Emmanuelle Thiercelin), 39 (Gail Mooney), 12–13 (Galen
Rowell), 27 (Nik Wheeler), 43 (Owen Franken), 30 (Philip Gould),
pp. 4, 4–5 (PicImpact), pp. 5m, 15, 36, 42 (Reuters), 40t (Sally A.
Morgan; Ecoscene), 25 (Sylvain Saustier), 34l (Thomas Hartwell),
pp. 11, 28–29 (Yann Arthus-Bertrand); Corbis Sygma pp. 21 (John
Van Hasselt), 14 (P. Franck); Getty Images pp. 5b, 24l, 29
(Photodisc), 42–43 (Stone); Harcourt Education Ltd p. 23 (Paul
Mason); Rex Features pp. 28 (Andy Paradise), pp. 18, 30–31 (Sipa
Press); Robert Harding pp. 38 (David Hughes), 6t (Travel Library),
pp. 5t, 8 (Roy Rainford), 40 (Ruth Tomlinson), 22 (Sylvain
Grandadam).

Cover photograph of an unusual angle of the Eiffel Tower
reproduced with permission from Getty Images/Photodisc.

Every effort has been made to contact copyright
holders of any material reproduced in this book.
Any omissions will be rectified in subsequent
printings if notice is given to the publishers.

The paper used to print this book comes from
sustainable resources.

Disclaimer
All the Internet addresses (URLs) given in this book were valid at
the time of going to press. However, due to the dynamic nature of
the Internet, some addresses may have changed, or sites may have
changed or ceased to exist since publication. While the author and
publishers regret any inconvenience this may cause readers, no
responsibility for any such changes can be accepted by either the
author or the publishers.

LONDON BOROUGH OF WANDSWORTH

501039237	
Askews	02-Mar-2006
C914.4 MASO	£12.50
	WWX0001390/0104

Contents

Where in the world? 4

Regions of France 6

The French landscape 8

Weather in France 12

Eating & drinking 16

Travelling in France 18

Countryside & coast 22

Life in the cities 28

Sport & culture 36

Tourist hot spots 40

Stay, or go home? 42

Find out more 44

France – facts & figures 46

Glossary 47

Index 48

Any words appearing in the text in bold, **like this,** are explained in the glossary. You can also look out for them in the Word Bank box at the bottom of each page.

Where in the world?

Skiing in the French Alps

Skiing has been popular in the French Alps for over a hundred years. Between December and April, millions of people visit the mountains to ski. Some just come for a weekend. Others stay the whole winter!

Your eyes (and ears!) open to the sound of cowbells. Blinking, you push open the shutters of your window and look outside. In front of you is a green meadow on a slope surrounded by woods.

To your left the trees drop down towards a distant **valley** bottom. In the haze you can see a little town, spread out along the edge of a river. To the right the slope climbs and climbs, until it rises so high it hurts your neck to look up. Mountains – whichever country you are in, it is in the mountains.

WORD BANK   valley area of low land between ranges of hills or mountains

Suddenly, a whooping, whirring line of three mountain bikers comes racing out of the trees and across the meadow. Just as they disappear into the trees, you spot that one of them is wearing a T-shirt with writing on the back: *Boulangerie de France*. At least you can guess where you are now: France. To be specific, the French Alps – home to the highest mountains in Europe. Now it's time to put on your Destination Detective's hat and find out more about this fascinating country...

Find out later...

What is Europe's highest mountain?

What caused these huge forest fires in 2003?

How far has this French banana had to travel to get to France?

A mountain biker rides down a trail at le Brevent, a mountain peak in the French Alps.

Regions of France

Lying on a desk in your room are a map, several photographs, and some notes left behind by other travellers. Whoever they were, they certainly knew about France!

France fact file

POPULATION:
60 million

AREA:
547,000 square kilometres (211,000 square miles) – the largest country in Europe

RELIGION:
Many people are Roman Catholic

LANGUAGE: French

CURRENCY: Euro

TYPE OF GOVERNMENT:
Elected National Assembly plus an elected president

Vendée – the Atlantic beaches of this flat land are a favourite with France's surfers, as well as with surfers from abroad.

Normandy – apples and pears are grown here. Some end up as delicious tarte aux pommes or tarte aux poires (apple tart or pear tart).

Paris – the capital city is home to over 2 million people.

WORD BANK   Basque group of people who have lived on the slopes of the Pyrenees Mountains for centuries. They have their own distinct language and way of life.

KEY
- ☐ Highest peaks
- ☐ Mid peaks
- ☐ Lowlands

0 ———— 150 km
0 ———— 100 miles

BELGIUM

GERMANY

LUX.

St. Malo

Normandy

Seine River

Paris

Brittany

Rennes

Vendee

Nantes

BAY OF BISCAY

ATLANTIC OCEAN

Central France

Loire River

FRANCE

JURA

SWITZ.

Lyon

Mt Blanc ▲

MASSIF CENTRAL

Rhône River

ALPS

Pays Basque

PYRÉNÉES

Toulouse

Provence

Nice

Marseille

SPAIN

ANDORRA

MEDITERRANEAN SEA

Corsica

DOMINICAN REPUBLIC

Martinique

Guadeloupe

Central France – around the Massif Central hills are regions such as Auvergne, famous for its amazing puys – the domes of ancient volcanoes.

Pays Basque – the western Pyrenees and Atlantic coast are home to the **Basque** people.

Provence – the limestone hills and beautiful gorges of Provence include the Verdon Gorge, a famous rock-climbing location.

Corsica – this Mediterranean island has lots of great beaches and beautiful landscapes. Every year, there are more visitors to the island than there are people living there.

Brittany – a beautiful coastal region, with fantastic beaches and hilly countryside. Brittany is home to many ancient stone circles.

The Métro

Paris' **Métro** subway was opened in 1900 and now has 14 lines, 211 kilometres (131 miles) of track, and 297 stations. No point in Paris is more than 500 metres (546 yards) away from a Métro station.

The French landscape

PARIS

You are here!

ALPS

N
W E
S

0   150 km

0   100 miles

Towering above your **chalet** are the highest mountains in Europe, the Alps. The Alps are about 15 million years old. Compared to the Appalachian mountains in the United States, which are over 400 million years old, the Alps are just babies!

The tallest mountain in the Alps is Mont Blanc (which means "White Mountain"). Mont Blanc is 4,807 metres (15,771 feet) high. Its slopes are always covered in snow above 2,400 metres (8,000 feet).

Mont Blanc

HEIGHT:
4,807 metres
(15,771 feet)

FIRST CLIMBED:
by Michel Paccard
and Jacques Balmat
in 1786

**PEOPLE KILLED
CLIMBING:**
over 1,000 people
by 2004

This is the summit of Mont Blanc, Europe's tallest mountain.

▼

WORD BANK   border line that separates one country or territory from another

The rocks that form the Alps once lay at the bottom of the sea. The two land masses on each side of the sea slowly moved together. As this happened, the seabed was pushed up between them, forming the Alps. Today the French Alps are part of the **border** between France and Italy.

Other French mountains

North-west of the French Alps lie the Jura mountains. The border between France and Switzerland crosses the Jura. The highest peaks are just 1,800 metres (6,000 feet).

To the west of the Alps is the *Massif Central*. This is the remains of ancient volcanic mountains, which have been worn down by the weather.

The Pyrenees mountains of the south-west separate France and Spain. Some of the biggest peaks here are over 3,000 metres (10,000 feet).

Alpine animals

Rare animals live in the Alps. The chamois, for example, is like a mountain antelope. The ibex is a kind of long-horned mountain goat. High up, golden eagles and lammergeiers make their nests. Lammergeiers are vultures that are also known as "bone breakers" because they drop bones from high up to break them open and eat the bone marrow inside.

Many people enjoy hiking in the Pyrenees because of the beautiful scenery and high peaks.

Rhône:
480 kilometres
(300 miles)

Garonne:
500 kilometres
(310 miles)

Seine:
770 kilometres
(480 miles)

Loire:
1,020 kilometres
(630 miles)

Little streams and great rivers

You don't have to walk far from your **chalet** to hear the sound of water rushing downhill. Little streams are everywhere in the mountains. In the **valley** bottom the streams join up and turn into fast-flowing rivers. Kayakers and white-water rafters love playing in these!

Many Alpine rivers end up feeding water into the River Rhône. This is one of France's greatest rivers. It flows from the Rhône **glacier** all the way to the Mediterranean Sea. The Rhône is the shortest of France's big rivers. Even so, it carries more water than any other.

➤
Thrill-seekers from around the world head for the rivers of the Alps in spring. The warm weather melts the snow. The rivers fill with fast-flowing water. Unfortunately, it's also ice cold!

WORD BANK   glacier solid block of snow and ice in a valley

The Garonne

The Garonne is another river that starts life in the mountains – the Pyrenees. It flows to the Atlantic coast. It goes past Toulouse, an important city, then past the city of Bordeaux.

The River Seine

The Seine is France's most famous river. It flows through the capital city, Paris. In the past, the Seine was an important transport route to and from the city. The Seine reaches the sea at the English Channel, near the port of Le Havre.

The River Loire

The Loire is the longest river in France. One-fifth of France's water drains into the Loire! The river flows from the *Massif Central* to the Atlantic Ocean. Floods were once common along the Loire. Today, its banks are lined with flood defences called **levees**.

The world's longest rivers

France's longest river is the Loire, at 1,020 kilometres (630 miles). See how it compares with the world's five longest rivers:

Nile (Egypt): 6,690 kilometres (4,160 miles)

Amazon (Brazil): 6,570 kilometres (4,080 miles)

Chang (Yangtze, China): 6,300 kilometres (3,915 miles)

Mississippi (United States): 6,020 kilometres (3,740 miles)

Yenisey (Russia): 5,870 kilometres (3,650 miles)

This is an aerial view of the Seine river, which also shows the *Île de la Cité*, Paris. ◀

levee bank, often made of earth, built to stop a river from flooding

Weather in France

Golden sisters!

Two of France's most famous skiers are sisters Christine and Marielle Goitschel. At the 1964 Winter Olympics they won gold medals in the slalom and giant slalom. Marielle announced she was going to marry French ski star Jean-Claude Killy. The news spread around the world before Marielle admitted that it had been a joke!

Mostly, the Alps are sunny and warm during summer. But if it was sunny when you woke up in your Alpine **chalet** this morning, there is no guarantee it will stay sunny. The weather here changes very quickly. People sometimes joke, "If you don't like the weather, wait an hour!"

A combination of heat, high mountains, and damp air allows thunderstorms to build up very quickly. After a clear morning, clouds can start to appear. They get thicker and blacker until suddenly the whole sky is dark. Thunderclaps boom along the **valleys**. Then suddenly there is a downpour. Unless you manage to get under cover, you will be soaked in seconds!

WORD BANK   abseiling using climbing rope to descend down a steep hill or cliff face

You wonder about the tall, tower-like structures you see on the mountainsides. These are ski lifts. In summer they sometimes carry walkers and mountain bikers to the higher slopes. But soon after the winter snow starts to fall in November or December the lifts are in action all day. Every week thousands of skiers go up the mountains on the lifts, ready to slide back down again!

So many people come to the Alps – for skiing, walking, climbing, and biking – that tourism is the region's biggest **industry**. Tourists even come in spring and autumn, when the weather is in between winter's snow and summer's sunshine.

Holiday fun

Hydro-glisse: swimming down a fast-flowing river holding a special float.

White-water rafting: six-in-a-boat mayhem! *Hydro-glisse* and rafting are especially fun when the snow melts in springtime.

Canyoning: climbing, jumping, and **abseiling** down waterfalls. This is safest in summer when flash floods are less likely.

VTT (*vélo tout terrain*), or mountain biking: brilliant fun on the sun-baked trails of midsummer.

While out hiking you are likely to meet people aged from seven to seventy!

This canyoner is hoping for a soft landing!

Elsewhere in France

What kind of weather would you find in other parts of France? In winter, northern France can be freezing, wet, and windy. It can sometimes be wet and windy in summer, too! Wise travellers take a waterproof coat, even in July.

Warmer south

Anyone looking for a break from the cold needs to head for the south coast, around the Mediterranean. Here, the summers are hot and dry. The average temperature in midsummer is about 24 °C (75 °F). Even in winter the temperature rarely dips below about 8 °C (46 °F).

Temperatures around France

The map and table below show the average temperatures around France in February and August:

City	February		August	
Lyon	6.7 °C	(44.1 °F)	27.6 °C	(81.7°F)
Nice	12 °C	(53.6 °F)	28.4 °C	(83.1 °F)
Paris	7°C	(44.6 °F)	25.6 °C	(78 °F)
St Malo	8.6 °C	(47.5 °F)	24 °C	(75.2 °F)
Strasbourg	5.3 °C	(41.5 °F)	26.3 °C	(79.3 °F)
Toulouse	11.5 °C	(34.7 °F)	28 °C	(82.4 °F)

▶ During winter, parts of northern and western France can be very windy, grey, and cold!

Eastern extremes

France's weather is more extreme the further east you travel. The city of Strasbourg, for example, is right on France's eastern **border**. Here the winter temperature is often below freezing, especially at night. But in summer, the average temperature climbs up past 24 °C (75 °F). All you need to pack then is a T-shirt, shorts, and flip-flops!

Wet in the west

Weather in the west is affected by the Atlantic Ocean. During winter, big storms race in from the sea. Rain and high winds blow travellers back to their hotels. But the storms bring big waves, so at least the surfers are pleased! In summertime the beaches are packed with holidaymakers enjoying the warm sunshine.

Heatwave 2003

In 2003, France suffered one of its worst heatwaves ever:

- temperatures rose to over 40 °C (104 °F)
- crops dried up in the fields
- the deaths of up to 13,000 people were linked to the extreme heat.

A forest fire in La Motte, southern France, was probably started by a campfire that got out of control, but the extreme heatwave allowed the fire to spread for many miles.

Eating & drinking

Food words

A few basic French food words come in handy for all travellers:

bread	*pain* (say "pan")
milk	*lait* (say "lay")
cheese	*fromage* (say "from-aje")
ham	*jambon* (say "zhom-bon")
butter	*beurre* (say "burr")
mustard	*moutarde* (say "moo-tard")

Walking around in the mountains is hungry work! There is a choice of places for travellers in France to eat:

- snack and sandwich bars, often with seats on the pavement
- cafés, where you can sit indoors or outside
- restaurants, where people usually sit indoors.

For a sit-down meal, maybe you would want to try one of the local **specialities**? In the Alps, these dishes usually contain dried meats, cheese, potatoes, and onions.

Eating out is popular in France. On average, people eat away from home every 3 days.

WORD BANK specialities food from a particular place

Table manners

Traditional French meals can last a long time. There are lots of courses (plates of different foods). You might start with soup, followed by fish. Next it could be meat, then a dessert, and finally some cheese! Adults usually drink wine with a big meal. Often people sit and chat for a while between each course.

Today this kind of long, traditional meal is less common. It might happen on a special occasion, such as Christmas Eve, or on a Sunday when family visit. On an ordinary working day, people are more likely to stop for a quick pizza or a sandwich lunch than a five-course meal!

Alpine specials:

Raclette: special cheese melted on to boiled potatoes

Pierre Chaud: a bag of boiled potatoes, raw meats, and a hot rock to cook them on!

Fondue: melted cheese for dipping vegetables or meats in

Tartiflette: a baked pastry dish with cheese, bacon, and onion.

People often enjoy a *fondue* after a day on the ski slopes.

The Alps are beautiful, but you cannot stay here forever. From the French Alps, you can reach Italy or Switzerland very fast. In fact, taking a wrong turn on some mountain paths can mean your walk ends in another country!

Your next stop, though, has to be the capital city, Paris. This is where most international flights leave from, and where the foreign **embassies** are based.

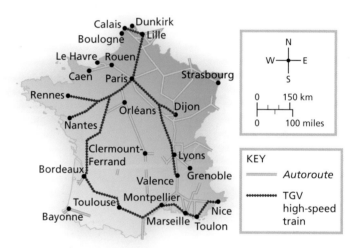

Terror in the tunnel

The Mont Blanc tunnel links France to Italy by road. In March 1999, a fire started in the tunnel. At least 30 cars were trapped, and 39 people died. The tunnel did not open again until 2002.

This is a memorial to the 39 people who died in the Mont Blanc tunnel disaster.

WORD BANK embassy place where another country has an official building

Getting around

Leaving the Alps by road is easy. The drive along the wiggly mountain roads can take a long time, though. Some roads pass through long tunnels. Others climb high **passes** before coming back down again.

The quickest way to reach Paris is probably by train. It is possible to travel by TGV – *train à grande vitesse* or "high speed train". These trains can reach speeds of 300 kilometres (185 miles) per hour, and the journey to Paris takes just over 4 hours. The TGV network links many of France's main cities (see map on p.18). It is also part of a high-speed train network that covers much of Europe.

Fastest thing on wheels

On 18 May 1990, a TGV train set a new train speed record of 515.3 kilometres (320.2 miles) per hour. This easily beat the previous TGV record of 380 kilometres (236 miles) per hour, which had been set in 1980.

Very fast TGV trains link together France's biggest cities.

Dangerous roads

France's roads are twice as dangerous as the roads in the UK and United States. This is largely due to the high volumes of traffic during August. This is when people are either going to, or returning from, their traditional month-long holiday.

Planes and cars

France has an excellent transport system. As well as taking the train, travellers find it easy to move around the country by car or aeroplane.

For long-distance car journeys, many people use the *autoroutes* (see map on p. 18). These are smoother and faster than most other roads. People have to pay to use the *autoroutes*. This means there is usually much less traffic on them. On shorter journeys most drivers use smaller roads.

Many French towns and cities suffer from **congestion**. At busy times the roads become clogged with traffic. This causes air **pollution** and health problems for people who live in the cities. Paris in particular is often very busy with traffic.

Traffic builds up quickly on the Champs Elysées in Paris. Some French cities have introduced trams to try and stop cars causing traffic jams.

WORD BANK congestion clogging or overcrowding, for example when there are too many cars on the road

Tunnel under the sea

France is connected to the UK by a tunnel under the English Channel. Trains travel through the tunnel day and night carrying cars and passengers.

Jetting around

All the big cities in France have large airports. Often these are international airports. Travellers can arrive at them from any part of the world. There are also lots of smaller airports. These may not have big enough runways for international aeroplanes. Instead people arrive at them from other smaller airports.

Car culture

Cars are popular in France:

- in 2000, there were 564 cars for every 1,000 people in the country
- in the UK there were 418, in Australia 530, and in the United States 760.

Cars drive off a Channel Tunnel train. The Channel Tunnel links England and France and first opened in 1994.

Countryside & coast

Oradour-sur-Glane

On 10 June 1944, during World War II, German soldiers surrounded the small town of Oradour-sur-Glane in Limousin. They killed all 642 people they found there. The town was then burned down.

Life in the countryside

Your journey to Paris passes through some beautiful French countryside. The Burgundy region, for example, is where some of the world's most famous wine is made. It is also famous for its delicious cooking. Charollais cattle are raised here – experts say these provide the tastiest meat in the world!

South-west of Burgundy is the area of Limousin. The hilly, wooded countryside here is not very **fertile**, but is very beautiful. Over the last 20 years, people from northern Europe have been buying homes in Limousin and other beautiful parts of France.

In the 19th century a devastating plant disease destroyed most of the ancient grapevines in Burgundy, many of which had been planted during Roman times.

WORD BANK   fertile able to produce many crops

New arrivals

Did you know that many wealthy people from northern Europe buy homes in France? One of the main reasons is that the cost of buying a house is lower than in many other countries. And of course, the weather is warmer than in England or Germany.

In some parts of France, these foreign buyers are having a serious effect. In Aquitaine, Provence, the Alps, and Brittany, for example, foreign buyers have driven the prices of houses up. They are now so high that local people find it difficult to buy a home in their own area.

The Basques

The **Basque** people live in the French region of Aquitaine, as well as across the border in Spain. Their language, *Euskera*, is like no other in the world. This makes it very difficult for travellers to learn!

You may see the sign "*a vendre*" many times on your trip as more French homes go up for sale.

"Local" bananas

The banana in your banana split in a French restaurant might have travelled thousands of miles to get there – but still be from France! This is because Martinique and Guadeloupe in the Caribbean are part of France. They **export** fruit all around the world.

Farming

Burgundy, which your train whizzes through on its way to Paris, is one of the richest areas in France. But other parts of the French countryside are poor. Many farmers have very little money, and struggle to make a living from their land.

Today, less than 10 percent of the population works in farming. Most French people work in **service jobs**. Many of these are based in towns and cities. Young people looking for work have moved away from the countryside in recent times. However, many are now moving back to the countryside. They travel to work in nearby towns or cities but enjoy a rural home.

This is a lavender crop in the Provence region.

European Union group of countries in western and central Europe
export sell to another country

Types of farm

Even though so few people work in farming, nearly 60 percent of France is used for agriculture. The average size of a French farm is just over 40 hectares (99 acres), which is twice as big as the average in the **European Union** as a whole.

Most large farms grow crops, such as cereals. Medium-sized farms often specialize in animal farming. They may be **dairy** farms, or farms where cattle are bred to provide meat.

Smaller farms usually produce specialist crops such as grapes to make wine. Some of these, especially the ones under 10 hectares (25 acres), are not worked full-time. The farmer can only make a living by having another job as well.

Huge fields are used to grow large amounts of crops in France.

Fried frogs' legs

Frogs' legs are a traditional French favourite, and farms produce millions of frogs a year to be eaten. This is a frogs' legs recipe for six people:

1 Boil twelve frogs' legs for 3 minutes, in water containing salt and half a cup of lemon juice.

2 Remove, dry with a clean towel, and add a little salt and pepper.

3 Make a batter out of two well-beaten eggs. Dip the legs in the batter and roll them in breadcrumbs.

4 Fry in oil until golden brown.

5 Remove and place in a folded napkin in a dish. Add fried parsley and sliced lemons.

These are some of the dishes hungry travellers find on restaurant menus:

Starter:

Assiette anglaise: a plate of cold meats, usually with bread

Soupe de poisson: fish soup, often with a spicy paste and cheese

Consommé: a clear, highly-seasoned soup

Fish:

Poissons de roche: fish caught among rocks by the shore

Moules marnières: mussels, cooked with shallots (little onions) in white wine

Langoustines à l'ailloli: saltwater crayfish with garlic mayonnaise

Farming seafood!

As well as raising crops and livestock, French farmers raise **seafood**. They grow it in the water, though, not in fields! In 1999, French fish farmers produced over 300,000,000 kilograms (660,000,000 pounds) of seafood. That's the same weight as about 2,222 blue whales – the largest animal on Earth.

Fish farming has increased because seafood is an increasingly popular food in France. Almost twice as much fish is eaten now as 20 years ago. Even in mountain towns like Chamonix you see fish and seafood restaurants.

Fishermen on a small trawler gather in buckets of crayfish to sell to local markets.

Fishing in the sea

France has 2,543 kilometres (1,580 miles) of coast. All along the coast are fishing boats – over 8,000 in total. Most of these are small boats that fish in the waters close to shore. The captains are often also the owners, and take the catch to market themselves.

Lakes and rivers

Freshwater fish are also popular in France. Most rivers have at least one old gentleman standing on the bank with a rod, hoping to catch his dinner! Among the fish that might take the bait are carp, salmon, trout, and bass.

Meat:

Choucroute: sausages cooked with cabbage and potatoes

Coq au vin: chicken cooked with wine, mushrooms, and onions

Boeuf bourguignon: beef stew with red wine, onions, and mushrooms

Dessert:

Bombe: layers of ice cream created in a mold

Crêpe Suzette: a thin pancake with a sweet orange sauce

Mousse au chocolat: smooth and creamy chocolate pudding

Most French fish farms raise shellfish as well. In total, they produce 30 times more shellfish than fish.

Life in the cities

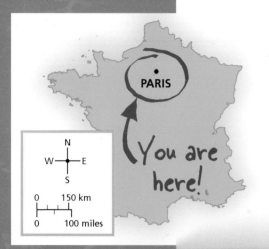

PARIS

You are here!

N
W — E
S

0   150 km
0   100 miles

The TGV train rolls into *Gare de Lyon* station. You have arrived in Paris, the capital of France. There's plenty to discover here! From *Gare de Lyon* you can catch a **Métro** train anywhere in the city. Where will you head now?

Le Parkour

Le Parkour, an activity involving running, jumping, climbing, and leaping but high up among the rooftops, first started in Lisse, on the outskirts of Paris. *Le Parkour* has been featured in several adverts and movies.

These *traceurs* – the name for people who take part in *Le Parkour* – perform risky stunts.

Paris choices

These are just a few of the places you could visit next:

- the narrow old streets of the Marais district
- Notre Dame church – made famous in the story *The Hunchback of Notre Dame*
- The *Musée d'Orsay* – a museum in an old train station.

Ups and downs

Paris is a very popular city. There are great museums, art galleries, markets, shops, and restaurants. The city is very beautiful.

Paris does have some problems, though. The middle of the city is very expensive to live in. Lots of people live outside the city and travel in to work. The traffic can lead to bad **pollution**. At the edge of the city are some areas of **poverty**.

During the 1800s, much of the middle of Paris was rebuilt. The city was organized around wide *boulevards* (streets).

The Eiffel Tower

Built: 1889

Height: 300 metres (985 feet), the first building to be taller than the Great Pyramid in Egypt

History: The Eiffel Tower was meant to be a temporary building. But in the early 1900s it began to be used as a giant radio aerial. It is still used as one today!

---

poverty lack of money, a good home, or enough to eat

School in the Caribbean

France has two overseas regions in the Caribbean. These are the islands of Martinique and Guadeloupe. Children here study exactly the same subjects as those in the rest of France.

This boy in Guadeloupe cycles to class in shorts and a T-shirt. He studies the same subjects as schoolchildren in France, but the weather outside is usually better!

Going to school

You decide to climb to the top of the Eiffel Tower to get one of the best views in Paris. The scene from its viewing platform is amazing on a clear day, because you can see right across the rooftops of the city.

Up on the viewing platform are crowds of schoolchildren. Luckily there seem to be plenty of teachers keeping control of them! France has about one teacher for every sixteen students. This is far more than in many other countries.

WORD BANK   compulsory something you have to do

Everyone in France has to go to school from six to sixteen years old. Most children actually start pre-school at three, though this is not **compulsory**. Children go to primary school until they are ten years old. Then they go to *collège* until they are sixteen. Only in the last year of *collège* do students have a choice of subjects.

At sixteen years old, students who are staying at school go to the *lycée* for three years. There are three different kinds of *lycée*. At the "general" kind, they might study literature or economics. At "technical" *lycée* they learn subjects such as science or technology. "Vocational" *lycée* teaches skills for particular jobs, such as plumbing or carpentry.

Back-to-front!
In France, children start primary school in form twelve, then the next year form eleven and so on. They finish school in *terminale*, or "finish."

At eighteen, students take their *baccalauréat*. This is their last exam at school. These students are nervously checking their final results on the notice board!

French cities

From Paris you could travel to any of France's other cities. Where would an adventurous Destination Detective go next?

Nantes must-see – Visit the Musée d'Histoire Naturelle and see the rhinoceros toenails and Egyptian mummy, among other treasures!

Toulouse must-see – Visit Cité de l'Espace, which includes a replica of the Mir space station that you can walk inside!

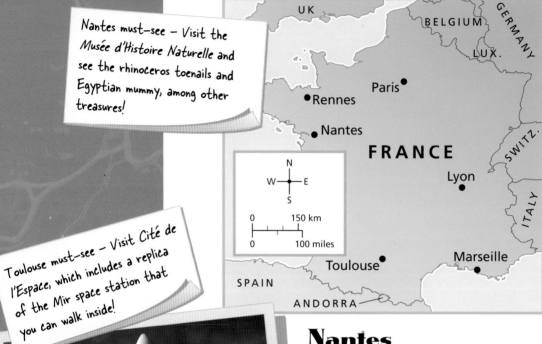

Nantes

Located at the mouth of the Loire River, Nantes grew rich from shipbuilding and trade. Today the city is an industrial and business centre.

Toulouse

In the south-west of France, Toulouse is one of the country's most modern cities. Toulouse has an ancient centre, but the city is known for its space and aircraft **industries** (see left).

Marseille

A Mediterranean port that has been a trading base for the last 2,500 years. One quarter of Marseille's people are Muslims, mostly from North Africa.

WORD BANK   catacombs tunnels used as burial chambers
funicular   railway that climbs up a very steep hill, pulled by cables

Lyon must-see – Use the **funicular** train to climb up to the town's Roman remains.

Marseille must-see – Visit the spooky **catacombs** of the oldest church in town, the *Basilique St-Victor*.

Rennes must-see – visit *Les Lices*, the tiny bit of ancient Rennes that survived the 1720 fire.

Lyon

Lyon grew rich as the home of France's silk industry. Then, after World War II, **petrochemical industries**, banking, and trade became important. Lyon is the headquarters of the international police organization Interpol.

Rennes

There are few very old buildings in Rennes, because in 1720 a carpenter started a fire that burned down most of the city! Today, Rennes is a trading centre and the capital of Brittany. Many local government jobs are based here.

petrochemical to do with petrol or natural gas

Bands to see

Many of France's **immigrants** live in the cities, especially around the edges of Paris. They have brought new music to France, including:

- "nu folk" bands such as *Les Négresses Vertes* (Algeria)

- rappers such as MC Solaar (Senegal)

- **rai** singers such as Cheb Khaled (Algeria)

- **griot** singers such as Mory Kanté (Guinea).

City life

About 75 percent of French people live in cities. What is life like for them? In some ways, it is like city life in any other country.

Good things

There are plenty of advantages to life in a big French city:

- there are lots of job opportunities
- the cities have plenty of great shops and restaurants
- there are sports halls, art galleries, cinemas, theatres, and museums.

Enjoying a relaxing cup of coffee and a chat is a popular pastime at France's pavement cafes.

Cheb Khaled on stage. "Cheb" is the name for young men who sing rai music.

immigrant someone who originally comes from a different country
rai music originally from western Algeria

Not-so-good things

Of course, there are also problems with living in a city:

- most people live in apartments rather than houses. French apartments are small, so living space can be cramped.
- buying or renting a home can be expensive, especially near the city centre.
- traffic can be a problem. Noise and **pollution** from cars fills the air, and cities such as Nantes are divided up by busy **dual-carriageways**.

Le Weekend

French people who live in cities like to escape on Saturday and Sunday for *Le Weekend*. In summer, camping is very popular. Families head for the countryside to spend a night or two under canvas.

French people love to escape the hustle and bustle of the city for a weekend's camping.

---

griot music common in western Africa. The griot is a storyteller who recounts cultural stories through song.

Sport & culture

Raid Gauloises

The *Raid Gauloises* started in 1989. In the past this race has combined running, swimming, cycling, map reading, and even parachuting! Each year, the race is in a different place. For example, *Raids* have been held in Patagonia (Chile), Costa Rica (Central America), and Oman (Middle East). The courses are so tough that many people feel it is the hardest race in the world!

➤

In 2005, American rider Lance Armstrong set an all-time record by winning his seventh *Tour de France*.

From the Eiffel Tower, the **Métro** can whizz you to another of the most famous sights in Paris – the *Arc de Triomphe*. After climbing the 280 steps to the top, you get to see a view across Paris.

Tour de France

In July each year, the *Tour de France* bike race finishes at the *Arc de Triomphe*. By the time they reach the finish, the riders have pedalled about 3,600 kilometres (2,235 miles). They are cheered along the last stage of the race by tens of thousands of people. The *Tour* is one of the most popular events in France.

Distance racing

Long-distance races of all kinds are very popular. Most people prefer to watch, not take part!

French people love long-distance yacht races. The toughest of these is the *Vendée Globe* race. The racers sail single-handed, non-stop around the world. No help at all is allowed. The fastest boats take about 90 days to make the voyage.

The French love taking part in sport too, of course. Hiking, skiing, cycling, and tennis are popular everywhere. Football and rugby are played and watched with great excitement, too.

Vendée Globe

"On the morning of the start, there were thirteen of us, not really knowing where we were going!"

– Sailor Jean-François Coste describes what it was like at the start of the *Vendée Globe* around-the-world race.

◄ Since 1989, the *Vendée Globe* race has started from the port of *Les Sables d'Olonne* on France's west coast.

Visit the Louvre

From the top of the *Arc de Triomphe* you can see all the way into the heart of Paris. At the end of the avenue is the Louvre museum, which is famous around the world. It holds one of the world's most famous paintings: the *Mona Lisa*. Wise travellers get there early – otherwise the queues to get in can be very long! If the wait is too long, what could you do instead?

Go to the cinema

About half the films shown in France are foreign, usually from the United States, but many French films are made each year. Even very small towns often have a cinema. Sometimes French films are big, international hits, like *Chocolat*.

These are the days when most people in France have a day off. Many of them are Christian holidays. There is usually plenty going on, but few shops are open.

1 JANUARY
New Year's Day

EASTER SUNDAY and **EASTER MONDAY**

ASCENSION DAY
40 days after Easter

PENTECOST
the seventh Sunday after Easter

1 MAY   May Day, a spring celebration

8 MAY   Victory in Europe (VE) Day, celebrating the end of World War II in Europe, in 1945

Opened in 1989, this fantastic glass building is called *La Pyramide*. It stands beside the Louvre Museum in Paris.

Listen to some music

Anyone who wants to go out and listen to music in France will probably have a big choice. On any night in Paris, for example, there might be Algerian *rai*, Senegalese singers, rap, electronic music from bands such as Air, traditional *chanson* (songs), live jazz, or classical music.

See theatre or dance

In summertime, street theatre is popular. The performers pass round a hat, and anyone who enjoyed the performance puts in some money. Indoors, France has many theatres showing plays, dance, and music performances.

More holidays...

14 JULY Bastille Day, remembering the French Revolution

15 AUGUST Assumption Day, another Christian festival

1 NOVEMBER All Saints' Day

11 NOVEMBER Armistice Day, this time celebrating the end of World War I

25 DECEMBER Christmas Day

31 DECEMBER New Year's Eve

◄ These two actors, one dressed as silent-film actor Charlie Chaplin, are part of a street theatre performance.

Tourist hot spots

On the seat next to yours on the **Métro** you find a folded sheet of paper. It turns out to be a map of "tourist hot spots". These are places in France that tourists love to visit.

Battlefields of World War I

Between 1914 and 1918, World War I raged in northern France. Over a million soldiers died in just one battle, the Battle of the Somme. Today visitors can walk through the fields and woods where the great battles were fought.

This war memorial was built in northern France to remember the Canadian soldiers who died in the Battle of Arras in World War I.

WORD BANK   abbey   building used by people who belong to a religious order
Norman   from Normandy, a part of northern France

The Verdon Gorges

Europe's version of the Grand Canyon, this amazing set of **valleys** and gorges is one of the most beautiful parts of France (see below left).

Carnac

Thousands of ancient standing stones line up across the landscape of southern Brittany. The stones have stood there for at least 4,000 years.

Strasbourg Cathedral

Made of pink sandstone, this fantastic building can be seen from all over Strasbourg (and most of the surrounding countryside). There are 332 steps leading to a platform with incredible views.

Avignon

Avignon was the home of the pope, head of the Roman Catholic religion, from 1309 to 1377. Today you can visit the *Palais des Papes* – the Palace of the Popes.

Mont St Michel

A famous **abbey** on an island, Mont St Michel (see right) used to be cut off from the land at high tide. Many **pilgrims** drowned trying to get there, caught by the incoming tide or by quicksands.

Lascaux cave paintings

Some of the oldest paintings ever found are on the walls of caves in Lascaux. They were discovered in 1940 by a dog – or at least, four boys who followed their dog into the caves.

Bayeux tapestry

The Bayeux tapestry is a strip of material that is 70 metres (230 feet) long. It tells the story of the **Norman** invasion of England in 1066.

Mont St Michel can be found on a rocky island just off the coast of north-western France.

pilgrim *person journeying to a holy place*

Stay, or go home?

So, you have been to the Alps, walked across the mountainous landscape and tasted the local food. You have crossed the heart of France and seen its countryside. You found your way to Paris. On your journey you have found out about the French lifestyle: how people live, what they eat, and the things they do for fun.

Still to do

These are just some of the things you could still try if you stay in France:

Learn to surf in Hossegor

Hossegor is the capital of French surfing. Every year there is a world-championship competition here. But there are easy waves for beginners, too!

Brazilian championship surfer Jacqueline Silva surfs the huge waves in the Hossegor world championships.

Now you have a choice. You can catch a taxi to Charles de Gaulle airport and board an airplane for home. Or you can stay – to explore the rest of France. There's plenty left to see and do. You could head for the Atlantic coast, the Mediterranean beaches, Brittany, Provence, the Pyrenees, or any of the other *départements* of France. Which is it to be? Stay, or go home?

Your airplane waits at Charles de Gaulle airport, ready for take-off.

A terrier gets a pat on the head from his owner for finding a huge handful of truffles in the fields of the Vaucluse.

Go truffle hunting
Truffle hunters use specially trained pigs or dogs to sniff out these delicious (and valuable) fungi. The world record paid for a truffle that weighed 850 grams (30 ounces) was set in 2004, and was £28,000 (US$54,000)!

Cycle up Mont Ventoux
One of the most famous climbs in the *Tour de France* race – even professional cyclists struggle up here. No wonder: the road climbs 1,610 metres (5,282 feet) in 22 kilometres (14 miles)!

Find out more

World Wide Web

If you want to find out more about France, you can search the Internet using keywords such as these:

• Paris
• River Seine
• The European Union.

You can also find your own keywords by using headings or words from this book. Try using a search directory such as **yahooligans.com**.

Films
Chocolat (2000)
This was a massive hit all round the world. A mother and daughter open a luxurious chocolate shop in a sleepy French village, which stirs up trouble with the villagers . . . at first.

Belleville Rendez-Vous (2003)
An animated movie about a French cyclist called Champion who is kidnapped while racing in the *Tour de France* and taken to America.

Are there ways for an eager Destination Detective to find out more about France? Yes! There are books, websites, and addresses to write to for more information:

The French Embassy

The French **Embassy** in your own country can give you lots of information about France. They can tell you about the different regions, times of the year for travelling, special events, and French culture. Many embassies also have their own website. In the UK you can write to:

French Consulate General, 6a Cromwell Place, London SW7 2EN.

One of the best embassy websites is for the French Embassy in the United States:

www.info-france-usa.org.

Further reading
These books are packed with exciting information about France:

Country Insights: France (Wayland, 1996)

France: Horrible Histories Special, Terry Deary (Scholastic Hippo, 2004)

Take Your Camera: France, Ted Park (Raintree, 2004)

The Rough Guide To France, (Rough Guides, 2004)

Timeline

58 BC to AD 476
Roman conquest of Celtic Gaul (part of what is now called France).

11th to 13th centuries
Agriculture and trade develop, and towns start to appear.
The royal family and the religious leaders are the most powerful groups in France. French knights travel to the "Holy Land" (which is now called Israel) hoping to drive out Muslims.

14th to 15th centuries
Epidemics (including the Black Death), famine, and civil war rage. Rivalry between France and England leads to the Hundred Years' War. Agriculture, the population, and trade all grow.

1610–1715
Louis XIII, then Louis XIV, reign.
Royal power is at its peak. France dominates Europe, and French culture spreads.
Start of large-scale sea trade.

1848–1852
Revolution in 1848 leads to a Second Republic.

1815–1848
Kings rule France once more.
The country becomes wealthier as modern **industry** starts to appear.
The first railways and colonies are established.

1799–1815
Napoleon Bonaparte rises to power and becomes emperor of France (1804).
European wars lead at first to France controlling much of Europe.
French armies then suffer defeats, and in 1815 Napoleon loses power.

1789–1799
French Revolution takes power from the king, then ends his right to rule altogether.
In 1793, the king is beheaded.

1852–1870
Louis-Napoleon Bonaparte, nephew of Napoleon I, seizes power, beginning the Second Empire.
France enters a period of strong growth and colonial expansion.

1870–1875
Franco-Prussian War leads to the fall of Napoleon III.
The Third Republic is established.

1914–1918
After World War I starts in 1914, northern France is invaded by Germany. The war ends in 1918 with victory for France and its allies.

1939–1945
France is defeated and occupied by German forces during World War II.
An Allied victory (8 May 1945) sets France free again.

May 5, 2002
Jacques Chirac is re-elected President of the Republic.

January 1, 2002
Euro bills and coins are introduced.
The euro becomes the currency of France, Belgium, Germany, Spain, Ireland, Italy, Luxemburg, the Netherlands, Austria, Portugal, Greece, and Finland.

1969–1981
France becomes a leading member of the European Community (later called the **European Union**).

1958–1968
The Fifth Republic
Crisis breaks out in May 1968 when students and many workers go on strike, opposing the government of Général de Gaulle.

1946–1957
During the Fourth Republic, France rebuilds itself after the war. Its colonies become independent. In 1957, the European Community is founded.

France – facts & figures

The French flag, or "Tricolour" (three-colour), was created during the French revolution. The three colours symbolize the monarchy (white) and the city of Paris (blue and red). It became the national flag in 1794, making it one of the world's oldest flags.

People and places

- Population: 58.8 million
- The French have more pets than any other nationality. 25% have one or more cats, 38% have a dog.
- Average life expectancy: 78.5 years

What's in a name?

- France's official name is République Française.
- France used to be called Gaul, but was invaded by the Francs in 400 AD, and has been called France ever since.

Money matters

- Before converting to the euro in 2002, France's currency was the French franc, made up of 100 centimes.
- Average earnings:
Men – £17,099 (US$30,022)
Women – £10,659 (US$18,715)

Food facts

- France produces 20% of the world's wine.
- The French make over 400 different types of cheese.

Glossary

abbey building used by people who belong to a religious order

abseiling using climbing rope to descend down a steep hill or cliff face

Basque group of people who have lived on the slopes of the Pyrenees mountains for centuries. They have their own distinct language and way of life.

border line that separates one country or territory from another

catacombs tunnels used as burial chambers

chalet type of wooden house common in the Alps

chanson typical French song

compulsory something you have to do

congestion clogging or overcrowding, for example when there are too many cars on the road

dairy to do with milk

dual-carriageway road with two lanes going in each direction, usually with a barrier down the middle

embassy place where another country has an official building

European Union group of countries in western and central Europe

export sell to another country

fertile able to produce many crops

funicular railway that climbs up a very steep hill, pulled by cables

glacier solid block of snow and ice in a valley

griot music common in western Africa. The griot is a storyteller who recounts cultural stories through song.

heatwave time of unusually hot weather

immigrant someone who originally comes from a different country

industry businesses that provide a particular service

levee bank, often made of earth, built to keep a river from flooding

Métro Paris subway train system

Norman from Normandy, a part of northern France

pass gap between mountains that travellers can cross

petrochemical to do with petrol or natural gas

pilgrim people journeying to a holy place

pollution release of harmful chemicals and other substances into the environment

poverty lack of money, a good home, or enough to eat

rai music originally from western Algeria

seafood fish, such as cod, and shellfish, such as crabs and mussels

service job such as banking, insurance, or working in a shop

specialities food from a particular place

valley area of lowland between ranges of hills or mountains

Index

air travel 21
Alps 4, 5, 8–9, 10, 12–13, 16, 17, 18, 23
Aquitaine 23
Arc de Triomphe 37, 38
autoroutes 20
Auvergne 7
Avignon 41

Basque people 6, 7, 23
Bayeux tapestry 41
Bordeaux 11
Brittany 7, 23
Burgundy 22, 24

canyoning 13
Carnac 41
Channel Tunnel 21
cinema 38
cities 28–35
climate 12–15
Corsica 7
culture 38–39
currency 6

driving 20, 21, 46

Eiffel Tower 29, 30
employment 24

farming 24–26
fish/fishing 26–27
food 16–17, 25, 26, 27, 43, 46

Garonne 10, 11
government 6

heatwaves 15
history 45

holiday homes 22, 23
housing 35
hydro-glisse 13

immigrants 34

Jura mountains 9

landscape 8–11
languages 6, 23
Lascaux 41
Le Havre 11
Le Weekend 35
Limousin 22
Loire river 10, 11
Louvre 38
Lyon 14, 33

Marseille 32, 33
Massif Central 7, 9, 11
Mediterranean 14
Mont Blanc 8
Mont Blanc tunnel 18
Mont St Michel 41
Mont Ventoux 43
mountain biking 5, 13
music 34, 39

Nantes 32
Normandy 6

Oradour-sur-Glane 22
overseas regions 24, 30

Paris 6, 7, 11, 14, 18, 19, 20, 28–29, 37, 38, 39
Pays Basque 7
population 6, 46
Provence 7, 23, 24
public holidays 38, 39
Pyrenees 9, 11

Raid Gauloises 36
regions 6–7, 24, 30
religion 6
Rennes 33
Rhône 10
rivers 10–11
road network 20
rural areas 22–27

schools 30, 31
Seine 10, 11
size of France 6
skiing 4, 12, 13
sport and leisure 4, 5, 13, 28, 36–37, 42, 43
Strasbourg 14, 15, 41
surfing 42

temperatures 14, 15
theatre 39
Toulouse 11, 14, 32
Tour de France 36, 37, 43
trains 19
transport 18–21
truffles 43

Vendée 6
Vendée Globe 37
Verdon Gorges 41

white-water rafting 13
wildlife 9
wine 22, 25
World War I battlefields 40

Titles in the *Destination Detectives* series include:

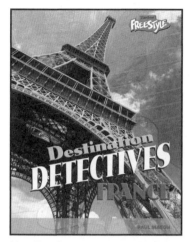

Hardback   1 844 21407 9

Hardback   1 844 21406 0

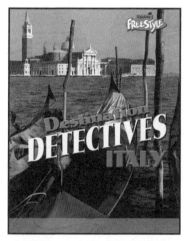

Hardback   1 844 21409 5

Hardback   1 844 21410 9

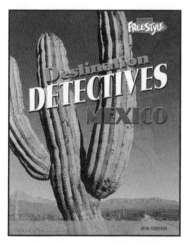

Hardback   1 844 21411 7

Hardback   1 844 21408 7

Find out about the other titles in this series on our website www.raintreepublishers.co.uk